www.finishinglinepress.com

# Carrying the Ocean

*poems by*

## Shymala Dason

*Finishing Line Press*
Georgetown, Kentucky

# Carrying the Ocean

Hoist your mind
To catch the wind.
Death can just stand on the shore
And gape as you go spanking by,
Sail full of the southern breeze.

Ramprasad Sen, *Grace and Mercy in Her Wild Hair*
*Selected Poems to the Mother Goddess*

## ACKNOWLEDGMENTS

"Dirty Shoes"—*Duende* (online), https://www.duendeliterary.org/shymala-dason, as
   well as reprinted from *Duende in The Literary Review*
"Ice-Skater"—*Redheaded Stepchild Magazine* Fall 2023 (online)
   https://redheadedmag.com/poetree/
"Invitation to Grief"— *RedHeaded Stepchild Magazine* Spring 2025 (online). A video
   poem of "Invitation to Grief" was a DEFF (Down East Flick Fest) Poetry/
   Spoken Word Official Selection
"Namaste"—*Santa Fe Literary Review* 2025 (online and print)
"On Encountering The Patriarchy One More Time"—*Grey Coven* Winter 2024

To the waters of this world that made their way into this book. To my late father who
held the foundations of my world firm and then walked into these poems as I wrote
them, and to my late mother, aunties, late grandfathers, old friends, and partners
who did likewise. To all my poetry communities, mentors, teachers and friends,
especially Malaika King Albrecht, Suzi Q. Smith, Aditya Surendran, my chapbook
group (Allison Burris, Ray Acevedo, Kathie-Louise Clarke), the Monday Night Poetry
community, the RedHeaded Stepchild Thursday book launch community, the All Our
Words critique group, and the various virtual SubDrifts (South Asian diaspora arts
open-mic communities) in which many of these poems were first shared with the
world during the pandemic. To Tara Sarath, who introduced me to SubDrift and who
is one of the most important compasses of my heart. To Joe McMahon, the sometimes
other half of my sketch, for website and video editing support. And finally, to you the
reader who holds this book in your hands. I thank you.

Publisher: Leah Huete de Maines
Editor: Christen Kincaid
Cover Art: Shymala Dason
Author Photo: Joe McMahon
Cover Design: Elizabeth Maines McCleavy

Order online: www.finishinglinepress.com
   also available on amazon.com

Author inquiries and mail orders:
Finishing Line Press
PO Box 1626
Georgetown, Kentucky 40324
USA

# Contents

## Ice-Skater

I see you, trembling on sharp blades
over a surface of unsettling, brilliant white.
You don't even know how to put the shoes on right.
Rubber slippers were enough
for where you came from.

Growing up walking beside salt-sweet surf
under coconut trees
and smelling bougainvillea and jasmine
in your mother's garden.
Thinking about dinner.

You'll have all your favorite things, at home.
Your mother knows what they are.
Along the way you would buy a coffee
foaming cream, and hot,
from a tin-roofed shack lighted only by a kerosene lamp,

while mosquitoes feed on the salt-sweet sweat
around your ankles and you nibble on a *jellabi*
as rich oil oozes onto your fingers.
But now, you have cold ankles,
in a cold country, and you're trying to skate.

But what if the ice breaks?

## Twelve Tins

I have to explain myself at customs
for carrying tea. But then, it *is*
twelve tins. Who does that?

But it's the best tea in the world,
you see. Only they don't export it
along with the export-type people

like me, the ones who wondered
what it would be like, elsewhere,
and would the shoes fit better?

They pinch, in Malaysia,
those nice-girl shoes,
are only safe if

—a big if—you color yourself
very small. Bear responsibility
without privilege, as here

in the West we export people
do too, though we didn't know
that would be the way of it,

nor that we would be without
real tea here: the best tea in the world
is the tea from Malaysia.

Please, all you people
from India and Sri Lanka
and China, please sit down.

I'm not trying to insult you,
only being homesick
for Cameron Highlands.

That's where the tea grows.
Roses as big as my whole face, too.
And, oh, yes, for the tourists a casino

where I once sat, simply, safely
in the middle of a winding, hillside road
with little traffic, in the long ago

as I breathed the air
and dreamed, foolishly
deeming that present not enough.

Wanting more
than the finest, golden tips
dancing in the sun.

Failing to value
until fifteen thousand miles
of world ocean came between

the precious taste
of that golden tea
that carries the scents of home.

# Namaste

*The father of an Indian daughter*
Who is doing well in America is excited
to receive a plane ticket, from a daughter
who says, '*Appa, please*
come and visit me.'
But then, once out of the airplane
in America, he sees his suitcase.

It looks different. Less.

Back home, visiting his parents in
their village (it's poor there),
taxi-drivers carrying that same suitcase
from the bus-stop call him, 'Sir.'
Now, in this American airport, he sees

his daughter's eyes hold embarrassment;

sees her thinking: *Appa* is not doing
so well as his daughter. What is he to do?
He's done: holding a baby. Saving. Praying.
Wishing a better life someday, for her.
Now he worries: because *he* never bowed his head before strangers.

*The daughter thinks, as she makes the call*
I have served flowers at holiday feasts
carrying a silver tray, jasmine
strands touching my fingers.
Sometimes my elders gave me saffron to hold
Or rosewater, to bless the head of the arriving guests.

Now, in this austere land: isolate, how will I
offer welcome? I cannot find the balm
of incense here, nor
holy saffron thread. There is no salt, no ritual
water. Only me. I am a vessel without ornament.

*Namaste*

**…ring around a rosie world…**

*ashes, ashes, we all fall down*

petals floating, soft wind whirling,
blood red, dropping from my hands

*One… Two… One… Two…*

a child's rhythm
singing, plucking:
he loves me, he loves me not?

petals floating, dying as they fall

*One… Two… One… Two…*

singing, hoping:
there is a garden full of roses
if this one does not satisfy.

ring around a rosie,
pocket full of posies

*ashes, ashes, they all fall down*

## On Encountering the Patriarchy One More Time

My body is full of thunder.

*Lightning. Storm. King Tide. Rage.*

It is full of fragility,
Tiniest seashell cast

*On tinier salt sand.*

Tiny dreaming in roaring surf,
Hoped for rocking in ocean arms

*Turned to shattering on rock:*

Under booted foot,
Mermaids cannot dance

*Without bleeding.*

## Childless and Dressing for a Date

I wear a Jessica Rabbit dress
though I'm not a bad girl,
only drawn this way.

My womb mocks me,
bleeds senseless preparation
for love that does not come.

I'm not so bright
or lucky,
but still optimistic.

I will wear red jewels
in my hair, to match the blood
that nourishes the seeds of my hope.

## Against Riptide

*A poetry of costumes,*
                    defining me.

        Pink-striped beach towel and multi-colored windbreaker:
        vacationer, relishing salt-swirl around my ankles, my toes.

*My winter-dry skin*
                    opening in gratitude,

        knees reddening. Meanwhile, a black costume, painfully
        self-conscious, waits to support a frightened performance:

*My artist's swagger*
                    at the center of the world.

        Aren't I cool, and hip and a lot of other tired masks?
        Uncertain poet, child of desire-driven diaspora full of

*Hopeful words:*
                    New York poet, writer, unanchored

        soul a little afraid. A little frightening. And so,
        another day, humble, I seek a different poetry.

*Different costumes:*
                    soft skirt, silk sweater, and ballerina

        shoes, worn delicately, to church. A nice girl
        in a room full of costumes, lamplight, and incense:

*Scent of chanting,*
                    whisper of billowing vestments.

        The breeze, like the breeze off the ocean, again a gift
        from God. And so, everything is all right.

## On Parliament Hill

I would have spent my life
sitting in the Lake Gardens
in Kuala Lumpur where I was born.

Under a tree
on those slopes sliding
down to the Lake.

The marsh green of it shallow,
artificial and yet,
town girl that I was

filled with nature
as I understood it.
The air mostly quiet, above,

for a town.
The bubble park,
traffic distant, or rare.

Occasional children's voices.
A man selling balloon animals.
Again nature, tamed.

Squeaky orange lion
without teeth,
as I was without skin

in that place.
My heritage blended
East and West,

illusion of balance, peace.
Palm trees and fir trees,
'Christmas' trees, we called them.

Native and other, together
Except for politics.
Outside the park

Up the hill,
Parliament Hill,
A curved overpass road

leading there lined
with fancy lamps
for importance.

The Constitution
practiced there
institutionalizing rights,

roles, by race:
'Some', and 'Other'.
And so I said,

"Goodbye," and left.
Not knowing
'Some', and 'Other'

was a Universal
Rule
everywhere

on the shores
of every ocean
of this world.

## And When the Storm Surge Settles

A New England cottage, with a strawberry-milkshake
pink porch floor at dusk, waiting,

dreaming of children playing in the garden,
laughter rising, to mingle with soft piano notes

celebrating counterpoint in sound
to the smell of muffins rising in the oven.

Hearing a heartbeat the small bones of my body
move. A new baby is born proving the Universe expands.

Overhead, a sympathy of geese labor nestward, circling,
every direction north: as the oven, breathing, warms the house.

## Mother's Day

Walk quietly.
My babies
are

with God,
sleeping.
They never woke

to day, today,
to sun on beach
or sound of

seagulls shrieking
on the wind,
or kiss of wind,

or touch
of mother-son sun
on their cheeks.

Walk quietly.
Please.
I am recording:

stories to tell
in Heaven,
lullabies to sing.

## Long Island Sound

Only the ocean talks to despair,
listens to silence
and slow footsteps.

Sliding, surrendering:
to fall again
would be to fall

not at all. Shards of pebble
and shingle cannot wound
feet already bleeding.

It's peace,
to bleed where bleeding
is allowed. Cauterized

by salt. Where none
contradict, and only
the seagulls watch,

unimpressed, as hermit crabs
dance amorous,
water-bound duets

and silent wind whip-burns my
skin, chills through to bones
and ache of wounded limb

and heart breaking, broken.
Stealing my voice: almost
amputee. Voiceless, I shiver, drop

tears, shaken,
into the welcoming, empty
silence. Long. Island. Sound:

The sloughing water
neither weeps
nor laughs, waiting

for me to speak tomorrow.
Whole again
perhaps. Tomorrow.

## When I Crossed the Ocean

They told me I was manic-depressive.
I'm not manic-depressive. Not crazy.

*I'm an immigrant.*

I have different rules inside my gut.
What to do and not do,
how people should behave,
what is the meaning of life:
all that.

It's too late to go back, though.
I've gotten used to American food.
Meat undercooked. No vegetables.

Going home to eat full-up Malaysian food,
chili and fermented fish,
and all the interesting parts
American butchers throw away
would be a bit tricky now.

It's a one-way journey,
this immigration business.
But everybody tells me I've done well,
coming to America. Only

there's this bi-polar nonsense.

One pole in America,

another on the far side of long oceans.

*So here I stay*
*Stomach*
*and heart and mind*
*all bewildered.*

### Icarus, in India a Girl

*The clouds in the sky come down in drops of rain, so as to surrender themselves to earth. Likewise, girls come on this earth, nobody knows from where, to get themselves bound.*
Rabindranath Tagore, *Lipika*

There is a south-Indian proverb that says:
*'If you aim for the sky, at least you'll go over the coconut tree.'*
But nice girls, everybody said, don't fly.
My aunties told me they were taught to walk
while looking down, modestly, at their big toe.

*'Toes,'* I pointed out, *'are less interesting than sky.'* But,

for my own good (that's what they said), they clipped my
tail-feathers.
No feathers, no flying, they thought. But
the feathers kept growing back.
They told me this was impossible. Yet,
*"Look! I am flying,*

*dancing, in the clear, cool air.'*

Only, what do you think, it's making me a bit nervous,
why is the ground getting closer?
*"Tsch! Tsch!"* voices—my aunties, all the aunties,
everybody's aunties—are waiting below me,
scissors in their eager hands.

*Please pray. I*
                        *am*
                *flapping*
                *as*
                        *hard*
                        *as*
                        *I*
                        *can.*

## Divorced, and Calling Home to Daddy

His voice cradles me
from ten thousand miles away
as it did when I was a child.

I am filled with tears.
He makes me laugh,
the poison of my grief

spilling
in a safe place
as he holds the foundation

of the world
firm.

## Never Mind

*In the end she runs away:*

Six airports, almost as many time zones. In Hawaii there is bird of paradise, and the dim shadows of the mountains against a greater darkness. Almost like the home she's running to, except that the mountains of home are gentler. Or perhaps she is lying to herself?

*Night train from Singapore to Kuala Lumpur:*

The train runs near the sea, salt in the air, passing villages with dirty water smells from puddles and old rain barrels. Chickens, motorcycles, fire smoke and latrines. Dogs barking, sleepy goats and cows. "*Allah u Akhbar!*" coming from the dark. "God is One, God is Great!" Houses outside waving from side to side as the coconut trees do; she falls asleep.

*In Kuala Lumpur:*

Eldest auntie says, "It's a very sad thing you've done, ahh!" Ladies sitting in a circle and *Never Mind,* and grunts of satisfaction. She has failed as she's been expected to fail, who does she think she is, every house has a doorstep, every marriage has flaws.

*Washington DC again, October:*

Autumn leaves whisper, voices lost against the sirens' screaming. She smells wet wool, virginal white and pure as she no longer is, drying in her kitchen; it's possible to wash wool.
She is not alive so she can't be dying. So why the sirens?

*On her finger, always:*

One ring, relic of lost life. Dark blue, a star sapphire surrounded by diamonds. She kisses it slowly, everything else gone: *never mind.* That's what they say in Malaysia.

*She is alone:*

Autumn evening blackness closing in. *Never Mind.*

## Visiting the Hairdresser

*After the style of Hafiz*

Being happy can be dangerous

People say, "Shymala is crazy,"
because I am happiest
walking in the rain.

I say, "Come. Walk with me."

They say, "No. Too busy. Important
things to Do. Stock market falling
savings vanishing. Serious times."

A man said—an incarnation of the Friend—

*"Consider the lilies of the valley..."*

Walk in the rain with me
and Consider; let the Friend
wash our hair

take away the pain inside our heads.

## The Color of Bones

I used to play on a rifle range when I was a child.
So safe I thought I was, in Malaysia
on the grounds of the military college where my father worked,
my child's hands tickling guppies
in the clear waters at the bottom of the monsoon drains
and, on an empty field with other children

tickling love grass not so many feet above bodies
in a WWII mass grave, hopeful
of finding bones. Gleefully terrifying ourselves
with speculation that some of those white,
knobbly stones in the field *were* bones. Not understanding
that the bones had been inside *people*

who had once walked, and talked,
and perhaps played, in that same field
before we came: played with our parents
before war came. Not understanding war.
Not understanding. Because it never flooded
when we children were down in the drains.

Young trainee soldiers carrying guns
and lonely for little brothers and sisters
gave us sweets, though sergeants (a sterner breed)
shouted at us. Or, worse sometimes, dragged us home
to be shouted at again by our parents, and of course
sometimes beaten in hopes of civilizing us.

Aunties said of me, "She's like a wild thing."
Which, you know, should really be a compliment.
It takes a little fierceness to survive.
So I ran away. First, down the road (at age four)
till my father came to fetch me home
with promises of tea, cake and understanding.

Later, I ran away to America, again sure of safety.
Land of the brave and the free they said,
"Liberty, Equality, Fraternity,"—no, wait,
that's someplace else, where they don't do it either.
And here, well, the best neurosurgeons in Texas
are threatened by ICE

because of the Brownness of their skins
and a Chinese doctor got beaten up
while buying PPE for his hospital staff
with his own money. The government wouldn't
pay for it, you see. And yet, they continue. We continue,
we Black, Brown, Yellow and 'Other' of us: in America.

Where it's not only young soldiers who carry guns.
Where people say, "He was having a bad day,"
about murderers, off the range,
who kill without understanding.
Without understanding their bones
are the same color as our bones.

And yet, skin matters: tickle the guppies,
see them swim over your hands, over your skin.
Watch the love grass close at a touch of your fingers.
Touch, skin to skin and heart to heart,
in white or black or every color in between.
Touch. Pray. Love. Understand. Continue. Please, continue.

## Dirty Shoes

I kicked a soccer ball in Malaysia;
they put me out of kindergarten,
in Kuala Lumpur, 1965, with aunties
praying over me in relays,
"Save this wild child."
Forty-five years pass. Aunties, those alive, unstoppable, praying
all the while.
As I sit in California reading email,
a primary school classmate now in Australia
tells me we had dirty shoes back then,
from kicking stones, with our mothers
mourning in a circle, "Ragamuffin daughters.
*What* to do?"
Emigration! Send them off to Europe, America, Australia,
tell your friends, "Daughter is Doing Well.
Overseas." Nobody can see her shoes.
Girls practicing soccer near my American home
are as grubby and sticky as any boys, ponytails everywhere,
bobbing, the only sign
they're actually girls: liberated—
nothing to do with jobs or voting,
our Kuala Lumpur mothers were right
about emigration. Benefits of overseas life.
Freedom to get dirty, that's *what*.
Running. Shouting.
*Playing.*

**For My Niece after the Oak Creek Temple Shooting**

"There was a mass murder of people who look like us.
You'll be upset, let me cook something for you."
Sounds crazy, no? But what's an Auntie to do?

Food is the code of love, the more the ghee, the more
the love. "Here, eat one more *jellabi*, just for me.
It's not oozing oil, what a thing to say, you're so thin, simply eat.

"*Dhall* and *roti, and saag* or *sambar*, and rice and pickles, and
my great-auntie's curry, just for you. It will make you nice and strong.
Bullet-proof, in fact, my child.

"Surrounded on the outside by the prayers of a hundred Aunties,
only good things can come to you now.
Coated so thoroughly on the inside with ghee and sugar

"and food from our hands that you will know
you are loved invincibly, unswervingly, and—let's be honest—
sometimes even annoyingly. But always loved. Even if,

"God forbid, a madman's bullet should hit you.
I am coming to the vigil tonight, for the shooting victims.
*Are you coming? Can I cook and bring you food?*"

## Invitation to Grief

Come to the ocean at Monterey, please
on a winter's day. It will be wicked cold.
Come naked anyway. I want to understand
all of you. Want to wash us all over

in the water, let breakers push us off our feet
then conquer the undertow of the riptide
or else be swept out to sea and drowned to
resurrect as something new.

Brown pelicans will swoop over us
seals dance in the waves ignoring us. See
tiny shorebirds scurry back and forth, busy,
not noticing us. We do not matter

to the tapestry of life: are only
one creature among many creatures.
Perhaps we will come out of the water with
a banquet, built together on driftwood fire,

of harvested salt-rich superfood greens
and accepted bounty of shellfish
that died to feed us.
I read this into the wind

knowing you can hear me,
being everywhere and nowhere.
Take on a body, Brown like me
with too much unruly hair, and

come. Crystalize yourself out of the wind.
Soften and warm into life. Speak with me.
Explain the riddles of absence,
Hunger, need,

where there is plenty all around.
An ocean of plenty.
And if you don't
the cold is bliss too. So, I tell you

I will practice feeling bliss in freezing. I tell you
do not mask the presence, immanence,
of that bliss with absences,
losses that mean, at the very core

there are things good enough to miss.
Worth the pain. Do not
dare try to make me forget this.
When you come, I shake.

Wind, no doubt. Or possibly awe:
knowing you have more power than I.
But knowing also the ocean will feed salt
life into me if we quarrel.

## August Rose

New England highway by the sea—Ocean, but in New England
it is sea. See? Absence of fuss, the road winding, scenic
See-ing there's time enough, no need for haste. On
the cliff slope falling into ocean—looking over,
drawn by heady seduction of sweet late
August fragrance—See? Blanket of
soft red stars, wild roses holding
on with thorns, the cliff too
steep to reach Over or Up
or Down. See? Holding
on, refusing to
believe in
Fall

*

## If I Live to be Very Old

I want a garden full of the scent of rain
and happy earthworms. And me within it
the happiest, earthiest one of all

swinging my *cangkul*, Malaysian shovel
on a long pole, up over my shoulder and down
to bite deep into the earth. Cutting the earth

the earthworms too. Don't worry: they thrive on it:
as my grandfathers thrived, despite the cuts of life
till they were old. And so shall I.

I want that. To grow as they did tapioca
that nourished our people through a war. Because
it's good to remember. Tastier vegetables, too.

Because it's also good to forget wars and rumors
of wars. Good to forgive. See: I will have roses, also.
I'll pick one, press its evening dew

on my third eye, then close the first two eyes
and pray. Ladies should grow roses to pray to.
My mother did. But her roses were fierce. Blood red

with hard, sharp thorns. Hers unto her alone.
Mine, softer, I learned to grow and share
A world ocean away from those first sharp roses.

It's almost evening now. Perhaps it's time
to return home again? Time to plant that last garden
if time permits. Time to remember all.

Time to forget all. Time to forgive.
Look, friend! Can you see, in that last garden, the sun
beginning to set? Take in the air! Quickly! That final scent

is roses breathing forgiveness into the night air. Can you
feel it? The blessed stillness comes. Mother? Are you there
in that silence? At the end, did the angels bless you?

Did they forgive, as I could not? Or is it forgiveness
enough that we tilled the earth, separately, decades
and miles apart inhaled damp soil and smiled? Is it

enough? We never fought in any garden.

## In Such Waters I Bless Myself

> *My heart, like a peacock on a rainy day,*
> *spreads its plumes tinged with rapturous colors of thoughts,*
> *and in its ecstasy seeks some vision in the sky,*
> *with a longing for one whom it does not know.*
> Rabindranath Tagore

(1)

Summer in Coastal Connecticut. The air is rich with
salt, moist with the promise of rain, and I am thirsty now. Alone.
Divorced. I drive to the beach, seeing everyone else is driving away
from it. There is only one other car there. One other Brown woman,
fellow monsoon daughter, lost like me. "I came to see the rain," she
says. "Yes," I say.

We share secret, trembling smiles. "Everyone else went away."
We raise our faces to the sky, our hair streaming and tangling in the
wind. Lightning flashes approach, then thunder, then rain that falls as
if God is washing the floor of Heaven with a river. We are wet to our
underwear instantly, and cling together, laughing with wet lips.

(2)

A friend has died. I walk in the morning mourning world.
There is birdsong, so many textures. Burbling water in a stream.
Runners sharing the wooden bridge I stand on. Life, pounding by,
step by running step, heartbeat by heartbeat. A million heartbeats.
And then gone. Yet the trees will shift in the wind and the birds still
sing.

(3)

I walk down by the water in Brooklyn for an eclipse that is
lost behind cloud cover and am blessed by a storm instead. Trees
swaying wildly in fierce wind, leaves rustling almost as loud as the
surf does. A nor'easter is coming. Foaming whitecaps cast spray in
my face. There no one visible in the mile or so I can see in either
direction. I walk and walk, body battered by a cold wind to the point
of exhaustion yet exhilarated, every cell tingling, as nature gifts her

29

wildness into me.

I'd learn to feed on salt wind, if I could do this every day.

(4)

Good Friday ashes on my forehead and contemplation of dust to dust. Oddly, the presence of my father, and others long lost. Life has savor, but dust when it comes will have its beauty too. For there shall be my father and my lost babies, perhaps.

And if oblivion, that too has Grace.

I should like to wear ash on my forehead all the time. It's powerful.

(5)

Dawn ocean, Asilomar, California. Ridiculous cold for the end of June, but glorious. It would be completely insane on every practical level to move here, where winter storms rip up huge trees and chunks of cliff, produce miles of flooded road and cut off the place for weeks, and yet potable water is always desperately short.

But on the level of soul and body, be still my beating heart. I'd live to be a happy hundred if I could ramble on these cliffs every day.

(6)

Atmospheric river is here. One of the few times California provides that rain-on-the-roof sound of my monsoon girlhood. It's quite lovely. On the other hand, there are probably going to be floods. I close my eyes, and remember brown water rising above my knees, the river behind my parents' home overflowing its banks, a tree as tall as a three-storey building uprooted and crashing down. Yet I listen to the sound of the rain and am comforted.

(7)

Power drop and the odd branch falling, but such a beautiful, beautiful sky. Sun meeting rain producing lights and darks so unexpected it is pure delight. A quiet walk down by the creek, the poppies are beginning and some are *huge*, maybe because of all the wet? The beginnings of carpets of tiny orange and purple flowers whose names I really have to look up. I discover those snails or slugs with something that looks like Disney turbans on their backs can manage in puddles, at least for a while.

(8)

Rain, and water in the creeks and catchment ponds. Geese and ducks playful, not strained. Water-washed world clean and sparkling. Colors extra bright. Every object—leaf, tree, bark, stalking cat or singing bird—richer, deeper, more varied to look upon. Each color now a dozen colors. Birds singing a many-voiced glee as loud as rushing traffic, but more innocent. New. Relieved. Renewed. Heron stalking frog as I walk by swollen waters.

(9)

Water-filled shingle puddle, so beautiful. Tiny, scrunchy-squishy, pinging sounds of water drops hitting stone, or inter-pebble water. Movement, soft, sinuous, sliding underfoot. Each individual grain free to move. All quiet around, so quiet I can hear the quietness, feel the quietness: I think nothing but puddle, and feel, just for a moment, absence of any grief.

## Monsoon Daughter

### (1)

It is midafternoon and monsoon season. I am home again, briefly, from America. I stand on my brother's verandah smelling the rain coming, while my family, inside the house, discuss a function we are to go to that evening. The air is heavy with the smell of the sea, healing absences so accustomed I had stopped feeling the emptiness of them until that moment.

My mother, mistaking shaken joy for grief, comes out and asks, "Why are you standing here? Come inside. Are you upset? We don't have to go to this function if you don't want to."

But I am whole. In that moment, I am whole.

### (2)

I remember her, a lifetime ago, urging me closer to her father's grave, thrusting a lit candle into my child's small hand. I am meant to plant it through the tangled blanket of smoldering wreathes into the friable clay beneath. We cannot take anything back from the grave, must light every candle. The air is dry and acrid with smoke as we plant more and more lit candles that tilt and scorch more greenery, on and on till black smoke drifts and the sky is no more, nothing left but choking dry air and sucking clay holding my slippers bound. I pull to escape, understanding dryness is death.

### (3)

Port Dickson, Malaysia, where I was born. I am surrounded by waters whose very names I love. Straits of Malacca. Indian Ocean. Andaman Sea. Bay of Bengal. Across the peninsula from me, the South China Sea is as warm and loving as a mother's womb, except in the fury of monsoon season. Beneath my feet as I bob in the water, the Sunda Shelf, a submerged continental plate, holds all of the lands around me together. The water is so shallow I could wade to Indonesia.

I laugh and take two steps, then suddenly flounder into a deep pool, sinking in over my head. Nothing is as easy as it looks. I scramble to shallow water again, while sand dollars, sharp as the thorns on my mother's roses, cut my feet.

(4)

Sunset, foam frothing against hard metal from the knife passage of the ship that I am on, Andaman Sea waters darkening from brilliant turquoise into sapphire mystery. Smell of the Purser's cigar, my father's warm, vibrating laughter as they talk together. We are crossing from Malaysia to India, reversing my parents' parents' long-ago migration journey.

Ahead of the ship the water sparkles with iridescence. People begin to cry, "Flying fish!" I see them, then, jumping improbably high and hovering in the air, carrying the ocean on their skin so they can stay in the air a while.

Spray blows onto my skin, and I understand, as the flying fish do: home is not the sky. I travel the world, jumping as they do, memories dripping through my cupped hands, salt tears and monsoon dreams and all those people who understood me not and ghosts of all the functions I have not attended.

(5)

Somewhere a child is lost to tsunami. Somewhere a liberty drowns in airlessness, somewhere sea turns from scenic to sardonic suffering. My World War II survivor father, a child who had lived through tsunami, laughs. Knowing another may come tomorrow, or even this next minute, he tells me about his lost best friend: then says, 'Look, there's a bird!'

And so shall I.

I carry ocean.

**Shymala Dason** is a first-generation immigrant from Malaysia to the US, and the child of second-generation immigrants from India to Malaysia. Her poetry naturally centers on belonging and unbelonging in family and immigrant life.

She has been published in *The Massachusetts Review, The Literary Review, Duende, The Margins,* the Asian American Writers Workshop (AAWW) war anthology, *Voices of the Asian American Experience,* and elsewhere. She has been shortlisted for the Flannery O'Connor short fiction collection award and longlisted for the Bath Novel Award and the Mslexia Novel Award.

She is an alumna of Bennington College and the University of Maryland and a former NASA tech. She is now a writing coach and developmental editor for fiction and memoir and also runs generative and critique writing workshops. She is a cancer survivor and a watercolor artist. The cover image on this book is a section of one of her paintings. *Carrying the Ocean* is her poetry debut. She can be found online at *https://www.ShymalaDason.studio.*